AF413832

Also by **WALLO267**

Books

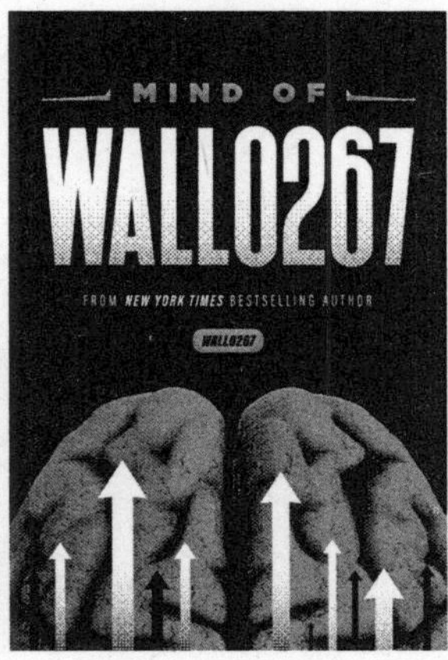

Audiobook Originals

The Mind of Wallo
Armed with Good Intentions

YES TO YOU NO TO THEM

YES TO YOU NO TO THEM

The Discipline of **SAYING NO** and the Freedom that Follows

WALLO267

HAY HOUSE LLC
Carlsbad, California • New York City
London • Sydney • New Delhi

Published in the United States by:
Hay House LLC, www.hayhouse.com®
P.O. Box 5100, Carlsbad, CA, 92018-5100

Project editor: Allison Adler
Cover design: Micah Kandros
Interior design: Jessica Angerstein
Author photo: Mike Dinerro

Hardcover ISBN: 979-8-3186-0595-6
E-book ISBN: 979-8-3186-0596-3

1st Printing

Printed in the United States of America

This product uses responsibly sourced papers, including recycled materials and materials from other controlled sources.

The authorized representative in the EU for product safety and compliance is Penguin Random House Ireland, Morrison Chambers, 32 Nassau Street, Dublin D02 YH68, Ireland. https://eu-contact.penguin.ie

Contents

This book is dedicated to
every person who is
going after their dreams
and to those who want to
but haven't yet.

May these words be the push,
the permission,
and the reminder
that you are worthy of
the life you imagine.

Say yes to you. Always!

Note from the Author

In a world that constantly demands more of us, more time, more energy, more compromise, it's easy to lose sight of who we are and what we truly need. *Yes to You, No to Them* is a necessary reminder that saying yes to yourself isn't selfish, it's survival. It's power. It's clarity.

This book is more than a collection of quotes. It's a guide to reclaiming your boundaries, protecting your peace, and choosing your growth unapologetically. Whether you're building a business, navigating relationships, or just trying to breathe deeper in your everyday life, these words will meet you where you are and push you to where you're meant to be.

Let these quotes ground you, challenge you, and most importantly, free you.

Here's to choosing you every single time.

Introduction

We live in a world that celebrates saying "yes" to everything—every opportunity, every person, every demand. But somewhere in that noise, we forget the most important "yes" of all: the one we owe ourselves.

This book was born from that realization. *Yes to You, No to Them* isn't about selfishness—it's about self-respect. It's about remembering that your peace, your power, and your purpose deserve protection. Because when you say no to what drains you, you make room for what grows you.

These pages are a mirror and a map. A mirror, so you can see where you've been compromising your worth. A map, so you can find your way back to yourself. You'll see quotes that hit like truth, words that challenge your patterns, and reminders that freedom starts the moment you choose you.

This is not just motivation—it's maintenance. A tool kit for your mindset, your boundaries, and your next level. So take your time. Reflect. Let the words work on you. And remember: The best thing you'll ever do for your future is honor your peace right now.

Say yes to you. Every time.

—**WALLO267**

How This Book Will Benefit You

This book was created to remind you of something simple but powerful: You are the most important "yes" in your life.

The world moves fast. Everybody wants something—your time, your energy, your focus. You give and give until you forget to ask yourself a basic question: *What do I need? Yes to You, No to Them* was written to help you remember the answer.

Each page is built to help you slow down, look within, and realign with what matters most. It's not about perfection. It's about progress. It's about building a version of yourself that feels grounded, clear, and unshakable no matter what's happening around you.

You'll learn how to protect your peace and stop apologizing for putting yourself first. You'll start to recognize the patterns that hold you back—people, habits, and distractions—and you'll gain the courage to release them. This book will teach you to say no from a place of love, and to say yes with conviction.

You'll also learn:

How to set boundaries that stick.
No more explaining, no more guilt. Just clarity, respect, and peace.

How to rebuild confidence.
When you stop waiting for validation, you remember who you are—and that's when you become unstoppable.

How to create a mindset built on growth.
You'll start thinking differently. You'll start moving differently. And you'll attract different results.

How to stay focused in a noisy world.
You'll learn how to tune out distractions, protect your energy, and stay consistent when others fall off.

How to walk in freedom.
When you finally say yes to yourself, you let go of the fear, the people-pleasing, and the limits that used to hold you back.

This isn't a book full of theory—it's a book full of truth. Real words. Real lessons. Real shifts.

You'll feel seen, challenged, and motivated to take action immediately. By the time you close the last page, you'll understand that saying yes to you isn't just a mindset. It's a movement. It's how you take your power back, protect your peace, and live with purpose every single day.

So take your time with it. Highlight what hits.
Revisit what hurts.

Because this isn't a onetime read—it's a lifelong reminder that you are worth choosing.

Say yes to your growth.
Say yes to your healing.
Say yes to your peace.

Always—
Say Yes to You.

NOTHING SHOULD EVER COME BEFORE YOUR PEACE.

Growth requires regular evaluation: who has access to you, who drains you, and who aligns with your future. Let go of what refuses to grow—no exceptions, no passes.

Protect your peace. No exceptions.

Growth demands constant self-checks.

You've got to ask yourself:

Who has access to me?
Who drains me?
Who truly aligns with where I'm going?

Let go of anything or anyone that refuses to grow with you. No exceptions. No passes.

Your peace is everything. It's your power source. When you have peace, you have clarity, energy, and momentum. Your mind moves freely. Your spirit stays light. Things flow.

But when your peace is disrupted? Everything feels heavy. That's why protecting it has to be nonnegotiable.

Start paying attention.
Who constantly brings negativity?
Who leaves you feeling empty after every interaction?
Who talks, but never uplifts?

You've got to be willing to remove people from your life without hesitation. Don't stall. Don't explain. Don't keep giving people access to your energy if all they do is drain it.

Growth is serious. Peace is sacred.

And nothing, absolutely nothing, comes before your peace.

GROWTH REQUIRES SACRIFICE. ACCOUNTABILITY DEMANDS DISCIPLINE.

Today's culture glorifies quick fame and avoids responsibility. Many cling to false dreams of stardom, avoiding work and independence, fearing they'll miss out. Yet they miss the true value of the success journey.

Everybody wants "overnight."

We live in a world that glorifies overnight success, as if it's the greatest thing that's ever existed. People chase the dream of becoming a star, of making it big, but most aren't willing to do the work required to get there.

They don't want to learn the fundamentals. They don't want to study the business behind the spotlight. They just want the shine without the sacrifice.

But here's the truth: Without real work, without effort, without education, you'll never experience true independence.

Some people don't actually want to stand on their own. They'd rather lean on others. They say they want success, but they're afraid to miss out on temporary pleasures—parties, friends, and distractions that add no real value to their lives.

And that's why growth and accountability never find them.

Because growth requires sacrifice. Accountability demands discipline.

At some point, you've got to say: *I'm ready to focus on what's important. I'm ready to do the work. I'm ready to take full responsibility for my future.*

That's the only path to elevation.
No shortcuts. No excuses. Just ownership.

YOUR DREAMS & YOUR LIFE BELONG TO YOU.

Stop letting people who ain't never believed in themselves stop you from going after what you want for yourself.

I come from an environment shaped by poverty, and even if you didn't, maybe you came from a space filled with negativity or constant discouragement. The common thread is this: In those kinds of environments, people often give too much weight to the opinions of folks who don't have anything real going on.

Think about it. The loudest opinions usually come from people who aren't doing anything. They're not building, not evolving, just watching. They have all the time in the world to criticize your moves, question your choices, and tell you what you "should" be doing . . . all while doing nothing themselves.

You've got to stay mindful of that.
Your dreams belong to you.
Your life belongs to you.

And what do you want out of this life?
It's only going to happen because of you,
not because someone else approved or
had something to say about it.

So forget their opinions.
Block out the noise.
Stay focused and keep pushing forward.

Growth
only happens when you align with what's
REAL.

Growth interference refers to the mental, emotional, or behavioral patterns that hold you back from evolving and reaching your potential. They stem from outdated beliefs, habits, fears, or attachments that prevent you from moving forward and embracing new opportunities or ways of thinking.

Growth interference is real and it's dangerous.

The danger in growth interference is that it keeps you stuck in a version of life that no longer exists.

You start seeing the world through the lens of outdated beliefs—beliefs passed down from your parents, shaped by your environment, or influenced by friends who never questioned anything for themselves. And because of that, you never stop to ask: What do I really want? What actually aligns with who I am today?

You can't grow when you're stuck clinging to ideas that are expired.

You're out there trying to navigate a world of flying cars using dinosaur logic, and it just doesn't make sense.

The hard truth is, a lot of what you're holding on to never worked for you in the first place. It didn't elevate you. It didn't elevate anyone around you. Yet you keep it alive, out of habit, fear, or loyalty to the past.

That's the interference. That's the block.

You can't evolve when your mindset is stuck in yesterday.

Let go of the outdated thoughts, the outdated conversations, and the outdated people.

Growth only happens when you align with what's real, right now and what's next.

NO to them &

YES to you

START MAKING YOU A PRIORITY

LIFE IS TOO SHORT TO BE PRIORITIZING EVERYONE ELSE'S NEEDS!

Priority: You.

Life is too short to keep putting everyone else's needs before your own. Every time you say yes to someone when your heart is saying no, you're abandoning yourself.

And let's be honest—most of the time, those yeses are going to people who are constantly taking. They show up with hands out, never pouring back into you. You keep giving . . . and giving . . . while quietly saying no to your own needs, dreams, and peace.

The truth is, you want to say no. You feel it. But you don't know how, so you silence your own voice.

You override that gut feeling. You betray your own boundaries.

But the question is:
When are you finally going to say yes to you?

Saying yes to yourself means loving yourself enough to stop letting people take advantage of your time, your energy, and your kindness. Because every time they come to you, they're putting themselves first, so why aren't you doing the same?

It's time to choose you. Say no to them.

Say yes to your peace, your power, and your priorities.

One of the most important things I've learned is that

WINNING AIN'T FOR EVERYONE.

Because the commitment to be disciplined is something most aren't willing to sign up for.

Winning ain't for everybody and that was hard to accept.

One of the hardest things I've had to come to terms with was realizing that some of the people I wanted to see win . . . didn't actually want to win for themselves.

I used to think everyone around me would rise with me, that if I believed in them enough, pushed them enough, showed them the way, they'd want it too. But I learned the hard way: **Winning isn't for everybody**.

Not because they're not capable. But because they're not willing. Winning takes discipline. It takes sacrifice.

It takes sitting out when everyone else is turning up.

It takes studying, showing up, and having an unshakable belief that you can become more than you are today.

Most people don't want that kind of pressure.

Most people don't want that kind of accountability.

So as much as I wanted certain people to win, I had to face the truth: They didn't want it. And sometimes, the people closest to you are the ones who simply aren't built for the journey you're on. And that's okay.

But once you accept that, you free yourself to move forward without dragging along people who were never meant to come with you.

Take accountability for your choices.

Unlock the life you want.

Your lack of availability & mobility is killing your ability to win in different departments of life! It's your fault you are where you are vs. being where you want to be in life.

Own the choices you've made.

The truth is, if you're not where you want to be in life, it's on you. You're not stuck because of anyone else.

A lot of people are trapped in relationships, friendships, and environments that don't support the future they dream about. And yet, they stay. They stay loyal to comfort, to routine, to people who aren't helping them grow.

But here's the hard truth: **You chose that**.

You committed to situations that are holding you back.

You tied yourself to people, places, and mindsets that don't elevate you.

So now, when opportunities come? You're not available.

You can't move.

You're not mobile enough to go where the next level of your life is waiting because you've anchored yourself to things that keep you grounded in the past.

That's not on them. That's on you. Blame you.

But also—**free you**.

Because the moment you take full accountability is the moment you start unlocking the life that's been waiting on you to show up.

Don't wait for corporate brands to look your way.

START YOUR OWN SHIT!

They'll beg you to partner or try to buy you out once you get your movement poppin'!

Stop chasing corporate validation.

Let's be real: A lot of corporate brands are completely disconnected from what's actually happening in the streets. They're out of touch with the people who really shape culture—fashion, music, tech, art, all of it.

So stop waiting for them to look your way. **Start your own shit**. Build your own platform. Create your own brand. Grow your own movement.

Because once you do? They'll either try to partner with you or throw money at you to buy in.

Too many people are out there kissing corporate ass.
Tap dancing. Hoping to get noticed. Begging for a seat at a table that wasn't built for them. And the wild part is:
You've already got what it takes. **You've got the energy. You've got the taste. You've got the vision.**

So what are you waiting for?
If you're saying you're hip, you're creative, you're tapped in, then own that. Start building something that's yours.

Because all that time you spend trying to convince people who don't even understand what's cool, what's next, or what's relevant . . . you could be building something that doesn't need their stamp of approval.

They're not the gatekeepers anymore, you are. So stop asking. Start creating. Own your lane. And let them catch up.

WAITING FOR THEM— Start YOUR MOVEMENT.

Too many people are stuck waiting.
Waiting on friends.
Waiting on money.
Waiting on the "right" time.
Waiting for someone else to cosign their dream.

"I need them to help me."
"When they get on board, I'll move."
"If they support me, I'll start."

Stop. All of that waiting is wasted time.

The truth is, everything you think you need from "them" is already inside you.
Your movement doesn't begin with their permission, it begins with your decision.

And here's the real kicker: The people who are meant to support, follow, and build with you? They're already out there, waiting on you to step up and lead.

If what you've got is real, if your vision is solid, people will show up.
But only after you show up first.

Create your own system.
Start your own wave.
And win with that.

Lead, and the right ones will follow.

Don't let past wounds make you suspicious of present blessings.

When naivety is gone, don't let paranoia take its place.

The truth is, a lot of people aren't naive anymore and it's because they've been hurt. Something happened. A betrayal. A loss. A lesson. And now that innocence, that openness, is gone.

But here's the thing: Being naive isn't always a bad thing. It's actually a beautiful space to live in. When you're naive, you're open. You're optimistic. You're not overthinking every move or doubting every intention. You let life happen without trying to decode it all.

But once life wounds you, that naivety gets stripped away and everything feels suspicious. Every good thing comes with doubt. Every new opportunity feels like a setup. You start questioning *Why me?* when something bad happens, and worse, you start questioning *Why me?* when something good happens too.

That's when you know hurt has turned into heaviness. You can't even recognize blessings when they show up. You're so used to pain that peace feels unfamiliar. You're so guarded that you see ghosts where there are none. You assume everyone's trying to get one over on you, when in reality, some people are actually trying to help you.

Don't let your pain from yesterday block your purpose today. Don't let your past rob you of your future. Let go. Heal. And allow yourself to believe in the good again.

FAKE **DEEP**

» IS THE ***NEW*** DEEP. «

FAKE **WEIRD**

» IS THE ***NEW*** WEIRD. «

FAKE **ON**

» IS THE ***NEW*** ON. «

FAKE **YOU**

» IS STILL SIMPLY BEING ***YOU.*** «

TRY IT!

Being you? That's still the realest thing you can be. Try it.

In a world full of trends and imitations, being yourself is rare and powerful. But it's not easy, because we're constantly fed the lie that if you just "figure it out" or play the part, you'll make it.

So when something becomes trendy, whether it's being "deep," being "woke," being "weird," or being "on," suddenly everyone wants to copy that. They start performing.

Used to be fake weird, now I'm fake deep.

Used to be invisible, now I want to be what's hot.

But the truth is, the most solid, unshakable thing you can be in this world is yourself.

Because when you're truly you:

- Nobody can expose you.
- You don't have to switch scripts when the cameras turn on.
- You don't have to pretend.

Being yourself is freedom.
And it's the easiest thing to sustain because it's real.
So stop chasing trends.
Start standing in your truth.

Just be you. Always.

When you grow, they're gonna say you changed. All because they love where they're at and upset that place of life ain't exciting to you no more!

Don't let them make you feel sorry,

KEEP MOVING UP

Growth is change.

But what they really mean is, "You stopped being comfortable in the same place I still am." See, some people get offended when your growth starts to highlight their stagnation. They'll say you're acting different, that you've switched up, but the truth is, they just don't like that you're not standing still anymore.

They were fine when you were stuck. They liked it when you matched their pace, their mindset, their comfort zone. But now? You're focused. You're leveling up. You're putting energy into your business, your peace, your education, your healing, your goals.

And they don't like it. Not because you're doing something wrong, but because it reminds them they're not doing anything at all. So what do they do? They try to reel you back in. Not with love but with guilt. They play mind games: **"You've changed." "You don't come around no more." "You forgot about us."** And now you're caught, trying to prove you haven't changed, while low-key slowing yourself down just to make them feel better.

But here's the truth: You don't owe anyone an explanation for evolving. You don't need to dim your light to make others feel comfortable in the dark.

Some people don't want to change. That's their choice. But you do. And that's your power. Keep growing. Keep moving up. And let them deal with their own discomfort.

READ

SPEND TIME

ALONE

EAT

CLEAN

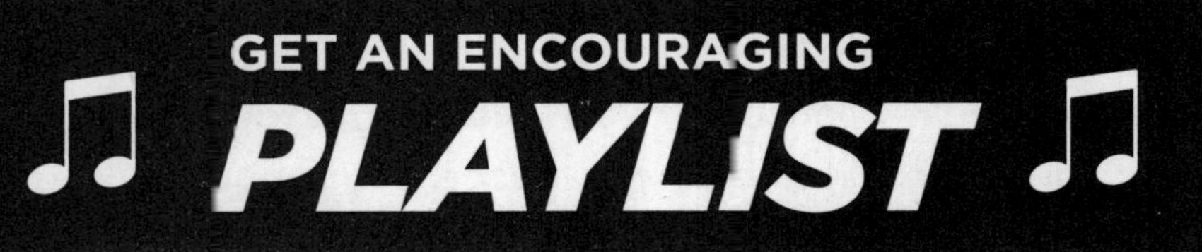

JOURNAL

RESEARCH

WORK OUT!

DRINK WATER

Do the inner work.

Research. Read. Journal. Build an encouraging playlist. Work out. Eat cleaner. Drink more water. Spend intentional time alone.

These aren't just habits. They're fuel.
They're how you raise your energy.
They're how you tap into your next level.

See, we spend so much time focused on what's happening outside of us. But the real shift? That happens inside.

Ask yourself:
What do I need?
What's missing in me?
What am I avoiding that could actually elevate me?

Start writing it down. Get specific. Then go after it relentlessly.

This journey is about self-mastery.
And that only happens when you commit to educating yourself, caring for your body, clearing your mind, and protecting your energy.

Once you make that shift, once you start doing that real, intentional work, it's over.

You're going to win.
Not because of luck.
But because you built yourself for it.

DEAR YOUNG MEN!

Establish yourself

BEFORE YOU DO ANYTHING!

Get you some consistency—cash flow, a job, a business, whatever! But make sure you lock you in first. Stop worrying about anything outside of your bank account, your own crib, and your car. Be someone you can count on—not your mama, not your girlfriend, nobody else.

Young men, focus on you.

I say that because I've been where you are. When I was young, I didn't focus on myself. I focused on everything outside of me. Chasing validation, distractions, and other people's opinions. That mindset led me down a dark path. It led me to prison. It led me to pain.

But it didn't have to be that way.

If you can lock in on yourself early—your mind, your goals, your purpose—by the time you hit your 30s or 40s, you'll be living a life most people only dream about.

Stop waiting for someone to come save you.
Stop leaning on people who don't even have their own life together.

Start building you.
Get out of your comfort zone.
Fix your credit. Get your license. Start traveling.
Expose yourself to different cultures, new ideas, and better ways to live.

The more you see, the more you know. The more you know, the more power you have to create the life you want. Start young! Because the earlier you start, the stronger your foundation will be. And when your foundation is solid, you'll be unstoppable.

This world is yours. But you've got to do the work. And it starts with you.

Dear young ladies,

Get your life in order before you chase love or approval.

Stack your money, find your peace, and build your own lane. When you're complete by yourself, no one can use love as leverage. Independence looks good on you.

Too many young women
are pouring energy into relationships,
friendships, and habits that drain
more than they give.

Real strength shows when you're anchored in your own lane.

With your own goals, income, and
peace, you stop bargaining your
worth just to be seen.
You stop chasing love that
costs your sense of self.

The moment you stop waiting to be rescued is the moment you start rising. Your energy shifts. Your standards sharpen. You move like someone who knows. The right people won't ask you to shrink, they'll meet you where you stand.

So build yourself.
Heal yourself.
Pour into yourself.

The woman who doesn't need permission
to feel valuable . . . she's the one who never loses.

One of the greatest businesses in the world is selling fear!

Don't buy it! Block out the bullshit.

Fear is one of the biggest businesses in the world—stop buying it.

They sell it everywhere: on your timeline, in the news, in conversations with people who don't even have their own lives together.

They'll have you believing in ghosts that don't exist. They'll convince you you're not enough, can't make it, or shouldn't even try. Don't fall for it.

Social media is the #1 fear dealer.
It's constantly trying to box you in—telling you what you can't be, what you shouldn't do, and why your dreams are too far-fetched. Fear, fear, fear. That's the product.

But here's the truth:
You can live an incredible life if you lock in on who you really are and what you're here to do.
Block out the noise.
Ignore the opinions of people who aren't living the life you want. Scroll past the fear tactics.

Every time you feed into that fear, you shrink your potential. But every time you choose you—your vision, your belief, your gut—you grow.

Stop watching the fear.
Stop sharing the fear.
Stop believing the fear.

You were meant to live free. So act like it.

STOP

OVER THINKING

STOP

CONTINUOUS PLANNING

Too much thinking, not enough doing.
Too many plans, not enough movement.

Everyone's stuck in endless cycles of strategy: Zoom calls, meetings, brainstorming sessions. But when it's time to actually make a move? Nothing happens.

At some point, you've got to ask yourself:
When am I going to stop planning and start doing?

You've mapped it out. You've talked it through. You've sat on it long enough. Now it's time to move.

This life is short. You don't live forever. But while you're here, you have the chance to create something that does. Something that lives long after you're gone.

But you can't build a legacy off of plans sitting in a notebook. You build it through action.

Even if you don't have it all figured out—move anyway.
You'll learn by doing. You'll grow by trying.
But you'll gain nothing by standing still.

Stop overthinking.
Start building.
Action > excuses. Always.

Privacy Protects PEACE

Privacy protects your peace.

When you move in silence and keep your life private, you protect your peace.

You don't have to deal with gossip.
You don't have to face constant judgment.
You don't have to manage people being all up in your business, trying to disrupt your energy.

Privacy is protection.

It creates a boundary between you and the chaos.
Think of it like a gate around your home, it keeps what matters most safe and secure.

Now, if you're a public figure, sure, there are things you have to share. But even then, there's power in choosing what stays sacred and what the world sees.

Not everyone deserves access to your life.
Not every moment needs to be shared.

The more you protect, the more peace you keep.

So guard your life like it matters because it does.
And privacy is one of your strongest forms of protection.

Stay healthy,

Stack your money.

Live on your terms.

Don't let anyone finesse you out of being you, especially not people operating from their own fears and insecurities.

I'LL SAY IT AGAIN: STAY HEALTHY. GET YOUR MONEY UP. LIVE ON YOUR OWN TERMS.

That's the formula. That's the focus. Because at the end of the day, you're responsible for you. And once you're locked in on taking care of yourself and surrounding yourself with the right people, you won't have to deal with the constant negativity of people trying to tear you down.

Let's get something straight: Health is wealth. It's your real currency. You can't chase dreams, care for your family, or enjoy life if you're not well. Want to watch the game? Travel? Build something meaningful? You need your health for all of it.

And the second half of the equation? Get your finances right. Because nothing in this world is free. Not even water.

Everything costs. So secure your bag and stop playing.

Lastly, protect your energy. Stay far away from anyone trying to pull you off your path. They'll try to distract you, drain you, or doubt you but that's not your burden.

Focus. Build. Move with intention.
And always, always live life on your terms.

MEETINGS DON'T MATTER.

Negotiating mutually beneficial terms and closing do!

Focus on results, not meetings.

Everyone's obsessed with meetings.
"Let's hop on Zoom."
"Let's schedule a call."
"Let's circle back next week."

It's like meetings have become the business
but they're not.

A meeting without movement is just conversation.
A great meeting doesn't mean a great outcome.

So the question is: Are we closing?
Are we negotiating real terms?
Is there an actual deal on the table? That's what matters.

Stop getting caught up in the hype of endless meetings.
Focus on results.
Focus on value exchange, solid terms, and finalizing deals.

The win is in the closing, not in the calendar.

People only gossip where ears are open.

If a friend listens to gossip about you, they're not your friend.

If people feel comfortable talking bad about you to your friends, your friends are part of the problem.

Let's be real. If someone can speak negatively about you to someone in your circle and feel comfortable doing it, that's because your "friend" gave them the green light.

People don't bring gossip where it's not welcomed.

So if they keep coming back to your friend
with drama about you, it's because your friend
has made it safe to do so.

That means they've formed a silent agreement
to talk about you behind your back.
It's a pact. A shared disrespect.

And you? You're looking at them like they're loyal.
Like they'd defend you. But in reality, they're sitting
at the same table with the people tearing you down.

Cut them off immediately.
Deny them access to your life, your energy, your presence.

Because someone who entertains disrespect
toward you is not your friend.
They never were.

Never let your ego stop you from doing what your heart is encouraging you to do.

Live fully and enjoy every day—because it might be your last.

Do yourself a favor: Don't let your ego rob you.

Never let your ego stop you from doing something
your heart is calling you to do.
Live. Move. Take the chance. Enjoy the moment
because tomorrow isn't promised.

So many times, we let ego talk us out of what we really want. It says, "Don't do that." Not because it's wrong, but because it's worried about how you'll look, how people will perceive you, or what others might say.

But here's the truth:
Your ego and your feelings are not the same.
Your ego and your intuition don't speak the same language.
And more often than not, your ego lies.

It'll finesse you out of amazing opportunities.
Out of love.
Out of peace.
Out of growth.

So don't ignore what you feel in your gut.
Don't silence what your heart knows is right just to protect an image that doesn't even matter.

Let go of the ego.
Embrace the moment.
And give yourself permission to live fully.

I truly wish you the best.

STOP BEFRIENDING PEOPLE WHO TALK ABOUT THEIR FRIENDS

If someone is comfortable bad-mouthing the people they call friends, what makes you think they won't do the same to you?

Think about it:

They have no loyalty, no love, and
no respect for the people closest to them.
Why would they treat you any differently?

If they gossip with you, they'll gossip about you.

Anyone who disrespects their own circle
is not someone you want in yours.

Get away from them immediately.

Don't abandon your dreams and talents for popularity.

Purpose will always outlast popular.

We're living in a time where people forfeit their dreams just to fit in.

Too many people are abandoning their purpose just to be seen as "cool" by people who don't even like or accept themselves.

There are people walking around with God-given talents, natural gifts that could change their lives. Maybe they're a skilled mechanic, a powerful background singer, a brilliant artist, or a creative mind with something special.

But they walk away from it.
Not because they're not good at it.
Not because it doesn't matter.
But because it's not popular.

We live in a culture that worships fame, celebrity, and influence. So instead of nurturing their gift, people chase clout. They trade purpose for popularity.
"I have something good, but it's not trending."
So they bury it.

Don't fall for that. What's popular isn't always purposeful, and what's purposeful won't always be popular.
But purpose lasts longer.

Honor your gift. Forget the hype.
And stop shrinking just to fit into a world
that doesn't even know itself.

Your comfort can become a cage.

Don’t let the fear of stepping into the unknown hold you back.

Choose opportunity over comfort.

You're so loyal to your city, you've caged yourself in.

The world is waiting on you, but you're too afraid to leave.

So many people fall in love with the comfort of hometown praise. They get attached to the love, the familiarity, the recognition. And because of that, they stay where it's easy. Where they're known. Where they feel important.

But what they don't realize is that they're holding themselves back. They're choosing comfort over opportunity. **Why?**

Because they're afraid.
Afraid they won't get the same support elsewhere.
Afraid of rejection.
Afraid of starting over in places where no one knows their name.

But staying in one place just because it's familiar can cost you everything that's possible.

Your gift deserves more than your block,
your zip code, or your city limits.
The world is bigger and so are you.

Don't let your loyalty to comfort keep you from stepping into your calling.

Stop chasing the spotlight.

Focus on doing great business, and you'll have a popular business.

Stop trying to be popular just because you have a business.

Be great at business so your business becomes popular.

These days, everyone wants attention just for starting something.
People launch a business and immediately want to be featured on podcasts, in interviews, or on the news—not because they've built something great, but simply because they've started.

But starting isn't the same as succeeding. Starting doesn't mean you've served anyone yet.
It doesn't mean your business is solving real problems, providing value, or delivering great customer service.

In today's culture, too many people chase fame instead of excellence.
They want to be known more than they want to be effective.
They want to be popular for having a business instead of letting their work speak for itself.

But here's the truth:
When you focus on building a business that actually serves people, one that's rooted in value, quality, and consistency, the recognition will come.

Let your business shine because it's great, not just because it exists.
Do great business. The spotlight will follow.

There may be 8.2 billion people on this planet, but you only need 5 to 10 yeses.

The key is aligning with the right people at the right time.

I'll share the story and who said yes when I get there. I'm 5 yeses away.

That's it. Just a few life-changing yeses. Not 8.2 billion. Not a million. Just a few.

And I say that because I've already seen it in motion. I've been in powerful rooms. Made major moves. And every win I've had so far came from someone saying yes, not a crowd, not the whole world, just the right person at the right time.

I've had way more noes than yeses. But the yeses I've gotten? They moved the needle. And I'm only a few more away.

Because of how my mind works, because of the way I build, because of the network I've created, I know I'm getting closer. My vision is becoming real.

But here's the catch:
Most people waste time chasing yes from the wrong people. They want validation from friends, family, their hometown, their followers. They want to be accepted more than they want to advance.

But financial freedom? Success? Legacy? That doesn't come from applause. It comes from alignment. And alignment only takes a few key people saying, "Yes, let's do it."

So I'm not here trying to convince the world. I'm just staying ready for those five to ten life-changing yeses. And when they come, I'll share the story.

Because that's all it takes.

FOCUS ON YOU

Stop worrying about people who don't like you. Stop trying to get accepted by people who don't love themselves. Put in the work needed to put you in the places you want to be in life!

Stop wasting energy on who you don't like or who doesn't like you. Stop seeking validation from people who don't even love themselves.

Focus on you.

Instead, put that energy into becoming the version of you that belongs in the rooms you dream about.

If you really think about it, most people give way too much attention to negativity. They focus more on haters, conflict, and critics than on the people who actually love, support, and believe in them.

It's wild how quick we are to spotlight the hate while ignoring the love.

But you only get one life. And spending it trying to win over people who don't even value themselves? That's a waste.

Redirect your energy. Double down on your growth.
And start celebrating the people who really ride for you.

Because they matter.
And so do you.

If you built something for yourself, stay on point!

Clout demons

(One who is willing to align themselves with everyone & do anything just to gain attention & popularity.)

are every-where.

If you've built something, protect it. Stay sharp.

We're living in a time where clout demons are everywhere.

Fake friendships.
Performative relationships.
People more obsessed with the attention they get from being around you than actually being with you.

Most folks aren't really for you, they're for what you can do for them. They want the proximity, not the partnership.

That's what a clout demon is.
Someone who will say anything, do anything, be anything, just to get attention. Just to attach themselves to your shine.

So if you've built something meaningful, something real, protect it.
Protect your name.
Protect your peace.
Protect your progress.

Because clout demons don't care what they destroy, as long as they're seen. Stay focused. Stay guarded. And never let the thirst for attention ruin what you worked so hard to create.

Appreciate when things go right in your life.

Enjoy the sun & stop waiting for it to rain!

Be grateful when life is good. Stop bracing for the worst.

Learn to appreciate the moments when things are going right. Stop searching for something to go wrong just because you've been conditioned by the pain of your past.

Too many people live in a state of constant pessimism, not because life is bad, but because they've been through so much that they expect it to be. They're always preparing for the storm, even when the sun is shining.

But here's the truth:
Just because it used to rain doesn't mean it always will.
Just because yesterday was heavy doesn't mean today can't be light.

Life can change.
You can have peace.
You can experience joy that lasts longer than a moment.

But you have to retrain your mind to believe that.
If your mind is always preparing for the worst, you'll miss the beauty of what's right in front of you.

So stop being stuck in survival mode.
Let go of the fear that something's bound to go wrong.

Yesterday is over. The sun is out. Enjoy it.

And remember: Change your mind, change your world.

Real value is earned through action, experience, and results —not assumptions.

Real value isn't based on who you think you are. It's based on what you've done.

It's earned through action, experience, and results.

The problem is, a lot of people walk into rooms acting like they're already the version of themselves they want to become. They move like they've arrived, when they haven't even started the journey.

They talk the talk, but there's no foundation beneath it. No wins. No work. No receipts.

It's all built on an illusion, an inflated self-image based on who they see themselves as in their head, not who they've actually shown up as in real life.

Confidence is important. Vision is necessary. But self-awareness? That's everything.

Before you demand value, deliver it.
Before you expect recognition, earn it.

Stop faking the arrival and start doing the work.

THIS IS **YOUR YEAR** TO → ACT → CREATE → CONQUER

THE FUTURE

BELONGS TO

THOSE WHO

MOVE!

The future belongs to the ones who take action.

Not the ones who keep planning.
Not the ones who keep talking about it.

You keep strategizing. You keep telling your friends. You keep cheering on everyone else who's doing what you dream of doing, wishing it were you.

So when are you going to stop watching and start doing?
When are you going to stop playing small?
When are you going to stop bullshitting yourself?

Nothing works unless you do.
Start now.
No more excuses. No more delays.

Get up. Get focused. Get moving.
It's your time. **Act like it.**

Go where the love and respect are abundant!

Stop wasting time convincing people of your value or what you bring to their lives. Instead, invest your energy in spaces and people who genuinely see you, appreciate you, and align with your purpose.

Go where the love and respect are real.

Stop wasting time trying to convince people of your value. Stop begging for acceptance in spaces that make you feel small.

You don't belong in any place where you're constantly overlooked, rejected, or questioned. You shouldn't have to prove that you're worthy of being in the room especially not every day.

Put your energy where it's reciprocated.
Be around people who see you, appreciate you, and genuinely want to see you win.
Align with spaces that support your purpose, not drain your spirit.

If someone makes you feel like you're too much or not enough, leave.
You don't need to shrink to fit.
Go where you're welcomed, not just tolerated.

Because real love and respect?
You won't have to fight for it.

Those who take action, even imperfectly, win more often than those who overthink and chase perfection.

Success favors the doers, not the over-analyzers.

Those who take imperfect action win more than those who overthink.

Success doesn't belong to the perfectionists.
It belongs to the doers.
The ones who move, who try, who learn as they go.

Everybody loves to plan.
They sit around strategizing, mapping it all out . . .
but they never move.
They get stuck chasing the "perfect time" or the "perfect conditions" and end up doing nothing.

Meanwhile, the ones they call crazy?
The ones who jump with no parachute?
The ones who say, "I'll figure it out on the way down"?

They're the ones who win.

Why?
Because action beats overthinking.
Every time.
You don't have to be perfect to win.
You just have to start.

This is your year of

SELF-LOVE

and "no" will be its anthem.

“No” is one of the most powerful words you can speak.

In fact, it can help you more than “yes” ever will.

Because real self-love means having the strength
to say no:
to people who drain you,
to places that don’t serve you,
to things that distract you from your purpose.

“No” protects your peace.
“No” guards your time.
“No” keeps you aligned.

This year, make “no” your boundary, your filter, your freedom. It’s the key that unlocks the path to the life you actually want to live.

Just so you know, you deserve that life.

People don't want what you give them; they want what you got! That's why nothing is ever enough.

Start leading with no!

People don't always want what you give. They want what you have.

That's why it never feels like enough.
Friends, family, associates—they keep coming back, not out of gratitude, but out of want.

You give your time, your energy, your help,
again and again, and still, it's never appreciated.
Why?
Because they're not just after what you're giving.
They're after what you represent.
They want your access, your opportunities, your light.
And the truth is, those things aren't theirs to have.

You're trying to pour into people who are chasing something you can't give them, you.

So here's what you do:
Start leading with no.
Set the boundary.
Cut the access.
Protect your peace.

Because once you stop letting people take advantage of you, you'll see things clearly. You'll realize the pressure wasn't love; it was entitlement. And when you cut it off, that's when everything begins to flow.

Let "no" be your filter. And watch your life get lighter.

IF YOU SACRIFICE YOUR HAPPY

TO MAKE OTHER PEOPLE HAPPY,

YOU'LL NEVER BE FUCKING HAPPY!

GO FUCKING LIVE

If you keep sacrificing your happiness for everyone else, you'll never be fucking happy.

Go live. For you.

You can't keep putting yourself last and expect to feel fulfilled. Stop worrying about everyone else because, trust me, they're not losing sleep over you.

Yes, if you have a wife and kids, take care of them.
That's your responsibility.
But even then, you still matter.

If being in someone's life means you have to bury your own joy just to keep them smiling, that's not love. That's self-destruction.

Eventually, the resentment builds.
You'll be angry at them.
You'll be angry at yourself.
And you still won't be happy.

So stop abandoning yourself to please others.
Prioritize your peace.
Protect your joy.
Because if you're not happy,
nothing else will ever feel right.

IF YOU DON'T LIKE WHAT'S GOING ON IN YOUR LIFE

REINVENT YOURSELF

It really is that simple.

If you're unhappy with where you are, who you're with, or what you're doing >> change it.

You don't like your relationship? Leave.
You don't like where you live? Move.
You don't like your job? Go get a better one.

But here's the key: You have to be willing to change. You have to be disciplined enough to pull the trigger on what's not serving you.

Too many people choose to complain instead of evolve. They stay stuck in situations they can change because it's easier to play the victim than it is to take action.

But the truth is: This is on you.

If you don't like who you are or
how life feels right now, then reinvent yourself.
Level up.
Become who you truly want to be.

You have the power to change your story.
But you've got to stop talking about it and start doing it.

Give her sun, great food, laughs & surprises.

One day it'll all make sense!

And this doesn't just apply to your partner.

This goes for your mother, your grandmother,
your daughter, your sister. Every woman in
your life who holds meaning.

Women love to smile. They love to laugh.
And more than anything, they love to feel loved.
So give them warmth. Give them joy.
Feed them well because food, good vibes,
and small surprises go a long way.

This is what it's about.
We're here to protect,
uplift, and show appreciation
to the women who show up
for us in so many ways.

Never stop reminding them
how special they are.
That's love. That's legacy.

We live in a world where everyone is choosing themselves.

Choose YOU!

Yeah, it might sound selfish.
But it's not. It's real.
Because the truth is, most people
are going to put themselves first.
Every time.

So you have to do the same.
In your daily life, in your decisions, in your energy,
you've got to ask:
What's best for me?
What supports my growth, my peace, my purpose?

And sometimes, the most selfless thing
you can do . . . is be a little selfish.

Because if you're not right,
how can you show up for anyone else?
You can't pour from an empty cup.

So stop feeling guilty for putting yourself first.
This world is real. It's hard. And the only way
to truly survive and thrive is to take care of you.

Because trust me. When the time comes,
most people will choose themselves.
So don't forget to choose you, too.

WITHIN THE INDUSTRY & OUT,

YOUR NAME IS ALL YOU HAVE.

SO

BUILD

your reputation wisely.

Your name carries the weight.

It's either spoken with respect or not at all.

Talent is important, but talent alone isn't enough.
How you move, how you operate, and how you
treat people—that's what builds your reputation.

Too many people try to cut corners.
They move shady behind closed doors,
thinking no one will notice.
But trust me, people talk.
And the things you think are hidden
always find their way to the surface.

Your reputation will follow you
further than your resume ever will.

So do it the right way.
Build with integrity.
Let your name hold value because
once it's damaged, it's hard to repair.

Play the long game.
Protect your name.

Locate your tribe.

Connect with like-minded folks.

Concentrate your time and resources.

Find your tribe.

Figure out who's truly with you and for you and then move with focus and purpose.

Like-minded people need to connect.
Your time, your energy, and your resources should only be shared with those who are locked in and aligned with the mission.

Once you know who your tribe is, build for them.
Stop trying to please everyone. Stop trying to be accessible to everybody. What you're building isn't for the world, it's for the movement.

When you let the wrong people in, they don't add, they take. They drain the energy. They dilute the vision. That's why you have to protect the circle.

Guard your tribe.
Guard your vision.
And understand that access is earned. Not everyone deserves a seat at your table.

Focus on your people, build with intention, and move like your future depends on it because it does.

Be selective —your elevation depends on it.

Growth is in your hands. But it starts with discipline and clarity.

You've got to understand that everything isn't for you.
Not every opportunity deserves your time.
Not everything that looks good is aligned with your goals.

If you're at level 5 trying to get to 10, then to 15, and beyond, you can't afford to chase every shiny thing that pops up.
You've got to stay focused.
You've got to be strategic.
You've got to say no to good so you can say yes to great.

Elevation requires intention.
And intention requires selectiveness.

Stick to the formula you've built.
Trust your plan.
Keep your eyes on where you're going, not just what's flashing in front of you.

Because the fastest way to delay your growth is by getting distracted.

But when you're disciplined and selective, your journey becomes undeniable.

Remember, personal hype doesn't mean success.

Personal hype can be motivating, but don't confuse it with success.

A lot of times, we gas ourselves up so much that we start believing we've already arrived. We walk into rooms acting like we've made it, when in reality, we're still on the journey.

Yes, self-belief is necessary.
Yes, confidence matters.
But self-created hype is just fuel, it's not the finish line.

You have to stay grounded.
Use your inner voice to push you forward, not to pretend you're somewhere you haven't earned yet.

It's okay to be proud of yourself. It's okay to dream big. But when you step into new spaces, show up as a student, not as someone who already knows it all.

Let your work do the talking.
Let your results speak louder than your words.

Because true elevation comes not from hype but from humility, growth, and action.

LEARN & RESPECT YOUR POSITION IN PEOPLE'S LIVES

and save yourself the resentment.

Don't give resentment a chance to grow.

Resentment often comes from expecting a level of access, treatment, or importance in someone's life that doesn't match the position you actually hold.

We get upset when we're not treated the way we think we deserve. But the truth is, the way someone treats you reveals your place in their life. Their communication, their effort, their consistency—those are the signs.

The problem is, we ignore the signs.
We hype ourselves up, thinking, *I should be a priority. I should matter more.*
But self-love doesn't automatically equal priority in someone else's life.

It's not about thinking less of yourself. It's about accepting the reality of your relationship with that person.

When you learn to read and respect your role, you protect yourself from unnecessary pain.
You stop expecting what they're not offering.
And you free yourself from the trap of resentment.

Pay attention. Accept the truth. And move accordingly.

Stop being mad at people because your dreams ain't working!

BE MAD AT YOU!

Your dreams belong to you.

Not your friends, not your family, not your boss, not your network. You.

Nobody on this planet is responsible for making your dreams come true but you.
So stop blaming others.
Stop saying, "I'm not on because they didn't help me."
"They didn't put me in the room."
"They didn't connect me with the right people."

That's not their job.
It's yours.

You're the one who has to breathe life into your vision.
You're the one who has to put in the work, apply the discipline, and stay consistent.
You have to build the momentum. You have to keep going even when no one's clapping.

Your dreams can only take flight if you give them wings. So stop pointing fingers and start putting in the work. Because the truth is: No one's coming to save you.

And that's exactly why you have to show up for you.

LADIES & GENTLEMEN

It's ok to sit out—you're not missing nothing.

Stay **focused** on growing personally & financially.

Everything will still be there! I promise you . . .

because I did it!

Trust me. I'm on the inside of what real success looks like. And I'm telling you, the parties, the trips, the photo ops, they'll all still be there.

We get caught up thinking, *"I have to be at this event," "I can't miss this party," "I need to be seen, to show up, to be part of the moment."* But in trying to be everywhere for everyone else, we forget to show up for ourselves. You don't have to attend every birthday, every wedding, every trip, every outing. Sometimes, the most powerful move is to sit out.

I did it. I skipped parties I was invited to because I couldn't afford to be there, not just financially, but mentally and emotionally. I stayed in. Cooked my own meals. Saved my money. Protected my energy. Because I knew where I was going required focus, not distractions. There's nothing wrong with saying: "I love you, but I can't make it." "I'm sitting this one out because my goals come first right now."

And if your people really love you, they'll understand. Discipline now creates freedom later.

So don't feel guilty for protecting your progress. Don't feel bad for saying no when your future is calling for a yes to yourself.

Sitting out isn't missing out. It's leveling up.

When someone disrespects you on social media

PAY ATTENTION TO THE "LIKERS."

When someone disrespects you publicly,
pay attention to the reaction, especially the likes.

On social media, disrespect is loud and revealing. When someone takes a shot at you, your loved ones, or even your associates, it can sting. But don't just focus on what was said: Watch who engages with it.

Be thankful for the bold ones who come out swinging, because in doing so, they expose the quiet haters.

We're living in a time where clout-chasing, tearing people down, and "exposing" others has become a twisted form of content. People build platforms by being messy.
But here's the gift:

When someone publicly disrespects you, they also invite others to reveal themselves through a like, a comment, a laugh, or silence that speaks volumes.

Now you know.
Now you see who was smiling in your face but couldn't wait for someone else to say what they were too afraid to.

Let the moment show you what's real.
Be grateful for the exposure because
now you can move with clarity.
No more guessing. No more false circles.

Thank the disrespect.
It uncovered everything you needed to see.

HATERS ARE YOUR MARKETING TEAM

Let Them Work

Haters are your unofficial PR team.

Let me tell you something about haters:
They talk a lot. And that's exactly why you should sit back, stay focused, and let them do their thing.

Don't respond. Don't defend. Don't explain.
Because while they're busy running their mouths, they're also doing free promo.

See, the funny thing is, haters don't just expose how much they don't like you . . .
They also introduce you to people who've never heard of you before.
They'll talk about you so much, people start getting curious.
And if you're really doing something worth paying attention to? They'll send traffic straight to your page, your business, and your brand without even realizing it.

You don't need everyone to love you.
You just need the right people to find you.

And guess what?
Your haters are out there dropping your name in rooms and timelines you haven't even touched yet.

So let them gossip. Let them hate. Let them market.

Because if your work is real, they'll end up leading the right people straight to you.

PLAY DUMB

Advertising your smarts will have people camouflaging their true intentions.

Play dumb—they'll expose themselves every time.

One of the smartest things you can do is not let people know how much you know. When you advertise your awareness, people get cautious. They start hiding their true intentions, adjusting their tone, and putting on a mask.

But when you play it cool, when you play dumb,
they get comfortable.

They think you're unaware.
They think you're not paying attention.
And that's when they slip.

They start revealing their true thoughts.
They expose how they really feel about you.
They tell on themselves, without even realizing it.

You don't need to confront them.
You don't need to defend yourself.
Just observe. Stay silent.
Let them show you who they are.

Because the truth always surfaces
when people think you're not looking.

Play dumb.
Stay sharp.
And let their actions tell the story.

It's not that they don't like you; it's that your presence is intimidating.

It forces them to step it up!

Your presence exposes their comfort zone.

When you're in close proximity to real success,
it does one of two things: It inspires you to level up,
or it intimidates you into insecurity.
See, it's not always hate.

Sometimes, your progress just puts pressure on people. It shines a light on what they're not doing, especially when you come from the same place, same background, same circumstances.

You're out there moving, building, growing and they're stagnant. And that comparison, even if unspoken, makes them uncomfortable.

Not because you've done anything wrong,
but because your growth challenges their excuses.

It's a mirror they didn't ask to look into.

And let's be real—some people don't want more.
They don't want the responsibility, the discipline, the pressure that comes with growth.

So instead of rising to meet the energy, they resent it.
Not because you're doing too much, but because they're doing too little.

Remember this: Your light isn't too bright, they just haven't adjusted their vision. KEEP SHINING.

YOU GOTTA CREATE YOUR OWN WORLD & PROTECT THE ENTRY »»

The life you envision, the peace you crave, the growth you're chasing—it starts with building your own world. A space that reflects who you are, what you value, and where you're headed.

But here's the key: Not everyone deserves access to that world.

Just because you built something beautiful doesn't mean it's open to everyone.

Your world is your sanctuary, your peace, your purpose, your foundation. And to protect it, you've got to guard the door.

Be intentional about who you let in.
Only open the door for those who are worthy, aligned, and respectful of the energy you've created.

Because your space is sacred.
Your world is yours.
And not everyone deserves a key.

Business is Business, not an emotional relationship!

Build, grow & exit!

Build smart. Move smart. Exit smart.

That's how you win long-term.

One of the saddest things to witness is a business that's already dead, being held on to way too long. I see it all the time—people clinging to brands that had their moment, but they missed the window to pivot or sell because they were too emotionally attached.

At its peak, that brand might've been hot. The clothing line was moving. The coffee shop was buzzing. The attention was there. But instead of scaling or selling, they held on, just to say, "I've got a business."

Now it's outdated.
The momentum is gone.
And they're still stuck in a time that doesn't exist anymore.

Business requires clarity, not nostalgia.
If it's time to rebrand—do it.
If it's time to pivot—do it.
If it's time to sell—let it go.

Don't let ego keep you tied to something that's no longer serving you.

The game is about strategy, not sentiment.

In life, there's God, then marketing.

Everything you know, love, want, or chase was marketed to you.

From the way you think to what you value,
someone or something influenced it.

You didn't just wake up knowing what car to drive, what clothes to wear, who to vote for, or what success should look like. Those ideas were sold to you.

Family, friends, media, your community:
They all played a role.
You were told what to aspire to, what to associate with status, what to chase to feel important or accepted.

That's the power of marketing.

Before you ever made a choice,
the narrative was planted.
So while God is the source, marketing is the system.
It shapes perception, behavior, and belief.

There's God. Then there's marketing.
Everything else flows from that.

LOVE DOESN'T HAVE A SPEED.

DRIVERS DICTATE.

The journey is defined by the connection.

Love isn't bound by time.
It doesn't come with a countdown, a milestone, or a schedule. It's a feeling, an energy, that can hit you before you even see it coming.

People often say, "Love takes time."
But that's not always true. Sometimes, the right environment, the right connection, the right moment creates something so real, so deep, so undeniable, that time becomes irrelevant.

You might find yourself thinking,
How did I get here so fast?
But who said love has to take forever?
Who made that rule?
And why do we feel the need to follow it?

Love is about alignment, not timing.
When it's real, you don't control it. You feel it.
It just happens.

Love doesn't come with limits.
Let it flow.
Let it work.
Let it arrive when it's ready,
even if that's sooner than you thought.

Coaches Last longer THAN THE PLAYERS

In most areas of life, the coaches outlast the players. Think about it . . .

Phil Jackson had MJ and Kobe. Icons in their own right. But while their playing careers had a time limit, Phil's influence stretched decades beyond theirs.

In my world, I deal with a lot of "players":
athletes, artists, public figures.
And while many shine bright in their moment,
few know how to transition.
They don't know how to go from being
in the spotlight to guiding it.

They stay stuck in the identity of "the player,"
not realizing the real legacy is built in the coaching phase.

Everyone gets a moment. But only some learn how to stretch that moment into a movement.
Those who evolve—from performer to strategist, from talent to leader—are the ones who last.

History proves it:
The players entertain. The coaches endure.
Choose your next position wisely.

Stop looking for people to believe in what you want for yourself!

The faith you're chasing starts inside.

Stop expecting people to believe in your vision. Most don't even believe in themselves.

You keep looking for outside validation for something that was planted inside of you.

But the truth is, most people don't know what they want for their own lives. So why are you waiting on their approval for yours?

Think about it.
How many times have you gone to friends, family, or associates for their opinion on something they've never even dreamed of doing?

You're asking people who've never built anything to believe in what you are building.
That's backward.

Your vision doesn't need outside confirmation.
It needs internal conviction.

Stop searching outward.
Start trusting what's already within you.
The belief you're looking for starts with you.
And once you lock into that, you'll realize you never needed their permission to begin with.

Sometimes the best way to learn how to fly is to simply jump.

Humans are real creative under pressure.

Everything I've done that pushed me to the next level happened while I was under pressure.

I didn't always know what I was doing.
I just knew I had bills to pay, people to take care of, and a vision for a better life.
But the path? Unclear. The steps? Unknown.

So I jumped. I moved without having all the answers.
And that's when everything started to align.

The pressure forced me to figure it out.
Trying led me to learning.

Action introduced me to the people, the information, and the environments that taught me everything I needed to know.

You don't learn everything first and then act.
You learn while you're doing.
But if you sit still, waiting to be fully ready, waiting to have it all figured out, nothing's ever going to happen.

Jump.
Move.
Trust that the wings will grow on the way down.

MONEY

GIVES

MONEY

TO MONEY

ENERGY

»»» ATTRACTS »»»

ENERGY

One thing I've learned in this game of life: Momentum is real.

When you have money, more money seems to find you.
Opportunities pop up. Deals land in your lap.
It's like the universe recognizes abundance and keeps feeding it.

But when you're broke?
It feels like everything slows down.
Doors don't open as easily.
You're pushing harder, but nothing's moving.

That's because money moves where it already sees motion.
It's attracted to flow, not desperation.

And the same goes for energy.
When your energy is right, positive, focused, powerful, you start attracting people, situations, and outcomes that match that frequency.
It's like a magnet. You don't have to chase it. It finds you.

Money and energy are both contagious.
They multiply when they're in motion.

So get your energy right.
Get your money mindset right.
And watch both start showing up for you again and again.

Stay aligned, stay ready, and stay in motion.

Understand the importance of Robin to Batman.

IT'S NOT ABOUT WHO'S LEADING THE WIN.

It's about winning.

The truth is, winning is ten times easier with a team than trying to do everything alone.

Too many people miss out on greatness because
they refuse to play a supporting role.
They don't want to be the assistant, the coordinator,
the right hand. They'd rather lose solo than win as part of something bigger.

But here's the reality: Nobody wins alone.
Not in business.
Not in sports.
Not in life.

Even Batman needed Robin.
Even Jordan needed Pippen.
Even the CEO needs a solid team behind them.

When an NBA team wins a championship, everyone gets a ring, not just the star players, but the coaches, the trainers, the medical staff, and the equipment crew. Everyone.

If your goal is really to win, then drop the ego.
Stop worrying about titles and start focusing on outcomes.

You don't have to be the face to be essential.
Play your role. Contribute to the mission.
And go get that ring.

Build a real relationship with your insecurities

BEFORE

you have a relationship with someone else.

Too many people rush into relationships carrying deep insecurities, hoping someone else will fix them, validate them, or make them feel whole.

That's not love. That's emotional dependency.
And it's unfair to expect someone else to do the inner work you haven't done.

Before you seek connection with another person,
take time to sit with yourself.
Get honest about what you're insecure about.
Where does it come from?
What triggers it?
How can you begin to heal it?

You can't keep hopping from relationship to relationship, dragging the same baggage with you, then wondering why things never work.

Heal first.
Grow first.
Be whole first.

Then go build something real with someone who's done the same.

Fly with builders, RUN from wing clippers.

It doesn't matter if it's a friend, a family member,
or someone you've known your whole life.
If they constantly speak negativity
over your dreams, it's time to create distance.

Wing clippers are the ones who always
have a reason why something won't work.
They've never tried it themselves,
but they're quick to tell you why
you shouldn't either.

"That's not realistic."
"Why would you do that?"
"It's not that easy."

These are the voices that plant doubt, not growth.
And if you're serious about elevating, you can't afford to
keep people around who are committed to playing small.

Surround yourself with builders, dreamers, doers, not doubters.

Protect your vision.
Protect your energy.
And stay far away from anyone
trying to clip your wings.

Real teammates cheer every win.

(Even if they're not the MVP.)

You don't need people on your team who only support the win when they're getting the credit.

Because real team players understand the ultimate star is the victory, not the individual.

Whether it's business, sports, or life, when someone starts pouting after a win just because they weren't the one in the spotlight, that's a problem.
They'll downplay the success, shift the energy, and start infecting the team with ego-driven frustration.

That kind of attitude kills morale. And if it's not addressed, it spreads.

Sometimes, you've got to distance yourself or remove those people completely.
Because if it's always about them, it'll never be about us.
And if it's not about the team, the team will never truly win.

Protect the culture. Protect the chemistry.
And surround yourself with people who celebrate every win.
No matter who scored.

Respect, understand & be realistic with where you're at in life before making demands.

You can't build a healthy relationship if you're not being real about where you currently stand.

Too many people show up to relationships with expectations that match who they want to be, not who they actually are. They lead with illusion, not reality. They demand partnership, provision, or support from a place they haven't even grown into yet. That's why so many relationships fall apart.

If you come in pretending you've already arrived at the version of yourself you're still working on, you're building on a foundation of falsehood.

And when you're not grounded in truth, you can't grow together. You can't communicate honestly. You can't face real issues with clarity because neither of you is dealing with what's actually happening.

Before you ask someone to build with you, be honest about where you are. Respect your current season. Do the work. And don't expect someone to play for a team that doesn't yet have the structure to win.

Truth builds trust. And trust builds everything else.

FUCK IF YOU DON'T LIKE ME, I DO!

You really think I care about your opinion of me when you haven't even figured out who you are?

We live in a world obsessed with approval,
people constantly begging for validation:
"Like me, like me, please like me."

And the moment someone doesn't, they fall apart.
They question their worth.
They lose themselves trying to win someone else over.

Nah. That's not me.
I don't need your approval to feel solid.
I know who I am. I like me. And that's more than enough.

Stop chasing people who haven't even
found peace within themselves.
Their opinion doesn't define you.
Your self-respect does.

So again. Fuck if you don't like me. I love me.
And that's what matters.

WEAR WHAT YOU ARE,

NOT WHAT THEY WANT

Real style is about individualism.

It's an expression of who you are, what you believe, and how you feel on the inside.

When I think about fashion, I'm not impressed by who can mimic the latest trend the best. I'm drawn to the ones who dress from within.
The ones whose outfits are an extension of their mindset, their energy, their identity.

You might wear a red shirt with purple pants, and someone else might say, "That's ugly."
But if it's you, if it represents how you see yourself, then that's style.

Style isn't about approval.
It's not about fitting in.
It's not about copying what the world says is cool.

We've drifted too far from what true style really is. We've turned it into imitation instead of inspiration.
But let's be clear: If you're just mimicking, you don't have style. You have fear.

Real style is fearless.
Real style is personal.
Real style comes from the inside out.

Take one step. Every day.

Just do something that will get you closer to your dreams.

It really is that simple.

Research.
Write it down.
Work out.
Make a call.
Practice your craft.

Whatever your dream is, show up for it daily. Even if it's small. Because those small, consistent actions compound over time.

Every day, do something that says,
"I'm committed to this."
Touch your dream.
Feed it.
Water it.

And before you know it, what once felt far away starts to feel real.

Consistency turns visions into reality.
One small move at a time.

Money is the most desired language—

LEARN IT!

Money speaks louder than almost anything in this world.

And anyone telling you, "It's not about the money," isn't being honest or isn't being realistic.

No, money isn't everything, but it's tied to almost everything that matters in day-to-day life.

Food on the table.
A roof over your head.
Tuition for your kids.
Gas in your car.
Health insurance.
Life insurance.
Basic security.

Let's stop playing games.
Money gives you options.
It gives you freedom.
It gives you the ability to take care of yourself and those you love.

If you don't understand money, you limit your voice in a world that runs on it.

So yes, money is a language.
And if you want to thrive, you'd better learn how to speak it fluently.

Your happiness is your responsibility—nobody else's.

Stop blaming your family, partner, or friends. Make the decisions in life that will introduce you to the happy you want!

Stop blaming your family, your partner,
or your friends for how you feel.
It's not their job to make you happy, it's yours.

You know what makes you feel good.
You know what brings you peace.
You know what drains you and what fills you up.

So make the choices that lead you there.
If something feels off, let it go.
If the energy's bad, remove yourself.
If you're not where you want to be, do something about it.

Happiness isn't handed to you. It's created by you.

Stop expecting others to do the emotional work
you've been avoiding.

Own your joy. Own your peace. Own your growth.

No one can do it for you.
It starts and ends with you.

QUIT SHOWING UP FOR NO-SHOWS

Why keep creating space in your life for people who have no intention of doing the same for you?

You show up with your time, your energy, your attention, but they never planned to give any of that back.

And yet, you keep giving.

Time is the most valuable thing you have.
It's worth more than money.
You can earn money back, but you can never get your time back.

So protect it.
Stop offering it to people who don't value it, respect it, or return it.

Give your time to those who show up for you, not just when it's convenient, but because you matter.

Be mindful of who you allow in your house!

Some people just want to get into your world to see how they can pull it apart.

People who show up only to take, observe, or drain your energy. People who want access to your world, not to support it, but to slowly tear it apart.

Be mindful of who you let into your house. And by house, I mean your life. Your relationships. Your peace. Your purpose. Your family structure. Not everyone should have access to that. Some people don't even realize it, but everywhere they go, they bring chaos. They stir confusion. They break what they didn't build.

And sometimes, those people aren't strangers.
They're friends.
They're family.
They're people you've known for years.

But if they bring no value, only distraction, division, and destruction, they don't belong in your space.

Protect your house.
Protect your time.
And only give access to those who truly respect both.

Winning is about putting in your own work.

Proximity to success does not equal success.

Winning has nothing to do with standing next to a winner. It has everything to do with doing the work yourself.

Just because you're in close proximity to success doesn't mean you're successful.
Taking a picture with a winner . . .
Partying next to a winner . . .
Being on a FaceTime call with a winner . . .
None of that makes you a winner if you're not putting in the work for yourself.

Social media has fooled a lot of people into thinking that access equals achievement. It doesn't.
Clout doesn't equal progress.
Proximity doesn't equal purpose.

Winning is personal. It's built on discipline.
It's getting up every day and grinding toward your own goals. It's doing the hard stuff when no one's watching, and showing up when it's uncomfortable.

Standing next to an athlete doesn't give you their stats.
Being around a boss doesn't make you one.

You don't inherit wins, you earn them.
So if you want to be a winner, get out of the picture and get in the race.

DEAR CREATORS

WITH A CELL PHONE YOU CAN

MAKE A MOVIE >>

RECORD AN **ALBUM**

Start a media company, etc.

START A PODCAST

START A CLOTHING LINE

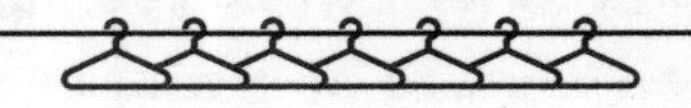

Who and what are you waiting for?

If you've got a phone, you've got power.

With the phone in your hand, you can make a movie, record an album, start a podcast, launch a clothing line, build a media company, create digital art, whatever you want.

So who or what are you waiting for?

I built everything I have starting with just a phone. The movement, the videos, the content—it all began right there. That little device in your pocket holds the key to information, connections, creativity, and resources.

You don't need permission.
You don't need the perfect setup.
You just need action.

You're already holding the tool.
Now use it to build your dream.
Let's go make it happen.

Uncommunicated Expectations

TURN INTO

Resentment.

So many friendships, relationships, and partnerships break down, not because of betrayal, but because of a lack of communication.

People get upset with you: family, friends, partners, coworkers, because you didn't meet expectations they never actually shared with you.

They had a vision in their head of how you were supposed to show up, what you were supposed to do, or who you were supposed to be . . . but they never said a word.

And now they're distant. Cold. Passive-aggressive. Resentful. You're left confused, wondering what you did wrong when the truth is, you just didn't read their mind.

That's the danger of uncommunicated expectations. They silently turn into disappointment . . .
then frustration . . . then conflict.

If you want clarity, speak up.
If you want peace, stop assuming.
And if you want healthy relationships, communicate what you need.

Because no one's a mind reader and silence breeds misunderstanding.

Know your craft. Know your worth. Don’t settle for less.

You get paid for what you know and played for what you don't.

The knowledge you have is what earns you income. The knowledge you lack is what people use to take advantage of you.

When you don't fully understand your value, your time, or the game you're in, you open the door for others to manipulate the situation.

They'll use your energy, your effort, and your skills without giving you what you deserve because you don't know any better.

And when you don't know your worth, you accept less. You get underpaid, overlooked, and undervalued, all because you haven't learned what you need to know.

So here's the key:
Educate yourself.
Know your value.
Master your craft.

Because if you don't, someone else will define your worth for you.

And they'll pay you in crumbs while profiting off your ignorance.

Every post is a reflection of your brand.

So be mindful.

One disrespectful post can close the very doors you're trying to walk through.

Social media might feel like a place to vent, but one careless or disrespectful post aimed at the wrong person can cost you everything.

People jump online to air out personal drama, take shots at others, or react emotionally without thinking about the long game.

But what they don't realize is this: The person you're dragging might be connected to the very people you hope to work with, collaborate with, or be seen by.

You don't know who's watching.
You don't know who's friends with who.
And in many industries, reputation travels faster than talent.

That one post, written in a moment of anger, can quietly block you from opportunities you've spent years chasing.

So be mindful.
Be strategic.
And remember:

Every post is a reflection of your brand, whether you mean it to be or not.

NEVER GIVE OUT SOMEONE'S PHONE NUMBER!

Never share direct access without permission.

Giving out someone's number, especially someone of value, is one of the quickest ways to lose access to them altogether.

If I gave you my number, it was for you.
It was tied to a specific reason, a relationship, a purpose, not for you to pass around to your friends, family, or whoever you think should have it.

Good connections are built on trust and discretion.
Just because you're connected to someone doesn't mean that person is now automatically connected to everyone in your circle.

Respect the boundary.
If someone trusts you with direct access to them, protect that. Don't risk burning the bridge by trying to play middleman for someone else.

Ask first. Respect the relationship.
And understand, access is a privilege, not a pass.

Dear ladies and young girls,

The biggest bag you can ever have is the one you create for yourself.

Own your power.

The most powerful thing you can ever do is build your own: Your own money. Your own vision. Your own path.

Because when the bag is yours, truly yours, it doesn't come with control, conditions, or compromise.
It's not tied to entitlement, emotional manipulation, or abuse—whether physical, mental, or financial.

This is something I constantly teach my daughter and my niece: The greatest gift you can give yourself is independence.

When you create your own, you don't have to follow someone else's rules.

You don't have to feel pressured to repay, submit, or stay in situations that don't honor your value.

You don't have to tolerate someone trying to control you just because they "did something" for you.

Especially as a young woman, you should never feel like a man has power over you because he holds the bag.
Hold your own. Build your own.
Protect your freedom by establishing your foundation.

Because the real power isn't in what you're given.
It's in what you create.

When a person becomes depressed because they can't be a part of the delusional lifestyle taking place on social media (parties, shopping, trips, relationships, success, dates, etc.). They worship a life they're not willing to work for.

MANUFACTURED DEPRESSION

Manufactured depression is real and it's rooted in illusions.

A lot of people are falling into depression not because of real-life struggles, but because they can't keep up with the delusional lifestyle they see on social media.

They scroll through parties, luxury shopping, vacations, relationships, and success stories, then start feeling like failures for not living the same life. But here's the truth: They're not depressed because life is actually bad. They're depressed because they can't participate in a fantasy they're not willing to be disciplined enough to work for.

The sadness doesn't come from reality.
It comes from comparison.
"I can't shop like that." "I can't go on that trip."
"I'm not in a relationship like that."
And instead of doing the inner work, they let the illusion consume them.

What they don't realize is this:
That depression isn't rooted in truth. It's rooted in envy, distraction, and avoidance. They're upset about a life they desire, but don't want to grind for.

Stop worshiping the highlight reel. Start focusing on the real work. And remember, your peace won't come from someone else's timeline. It'll come from the life you build, brick by brick.

Stop worrying about what everyone else is doing!

Simply go design the world you want for you.

Design the world you want.

Take a step back and have a real conversation
with yourself:
What do I truly want for my life?
Not what's trending.
Not what looks good online.
Not what other people expect.

Once you figure that out, go build it.
Create the life that reflects your values,
your passions, and your purpose.

Everyone's path is different.
We don't all want the same things.
We're not all headed to the same destination.

So stop comparing.
Stop watching everyone else's moves.
Start focusing on what you need to do
to create the life that fulfills you.

Your world is waiting. Go design it.

You've Changed!

I KNOW!

Growth looks like distance to those who stand still.

People love to say you've changed . . .

when they can't access you the way they used to
and they can't take advantage of your time,
your energy, or your presence.

"You don't come around no more."
"You're always working now."
Yeah, I changed my priorities.
I changed my mindset.
I changed my focus. I had to.

I've got responsibilities now.
I've got a purpose to fulfill.
I've got a family to take care of.
Chilling and staying the same wasn't going to get me there.

The truth is, I didn't change on you. I evolved for me.
And if you're still standing in the same place,
of course it feels like I moved.
Because I did.

Growth isn't personal. It's necessary.
And if elevation looks like distance,
that's just part of the process.

EMPOWER YOURSELF BY FOCUSING ON WHAT YOU CAN CONTROL.

When you fully accept and comprehend that everyone prioritizes their own well-being, you'll navigate life's challenges with remarkable ease! I wish you the best!

Focus on what you can control.

The key to peace and progress is simple:
Stop trying to manage everything outside of you
and start mastering what's within you.

It's your responsibility to prioritize you.
Not other people's choices.
Not their opinions. Not their timelines.

Everyone's going to put themselves first,
so it's time you do the same.
When you shift your energy toward your growth, your mindset, your discipline, and your goals, you take your power back.

And when challenges show up, as they always do,
you'll move through them with clarity and confidence.

Stay focused. Stay grounded.
And remember: Control what's yours,
and release what's not.

That's how you win.

KNOW WHO'S AROUND YOU AND WHY THEY'RE AROUND YOU

It's not enough to just have people around you. You need to understand why they're there.

Some people are in your life because they genuinely value who you are. Others might just like the way you move, the access you have, or how you make them feel.
And some? They're simply around for convenience—partying, vibes, or what they can get.

There's nothing wrong with that, as long as you're aware. Because when you're clear on people's purpose in your life, you can manage your energy, expectations, and boundaries.

Too often, we let friends, family, and associates in without asking the deeper question:
What role are they really playing in my life?

Don't be naive with access.
Be aware.
Be intentional.

You don't need to cut everyone off,
just know their position.
And act accordingly.

If you didn't appreciate her before she became who she is, don't expect a place beside her now.

When a woman grows, heals, and steps fully into herself, her standards, mindset, and boundaries all begin to change.

She's no longer moved by the same things, and she doesn't entertain what she once tolerated.

A lot of men had access to women before they truly knew who they were. But once she matures—through life, lessons, heartbreak, and experience—that same access disappears.

Because now?
She sees through the games.
She respects herself differently.
She honors her time and energy on a whole new level.

And truthfully, some women look back and regret ever giving certain people a chance.
Not out of bitterness but because they've grown.

So understand this:
The woman you once knew isn't the woman she is now.
And if you didn't value her before she evolved, don't expect to stand beside her now that she has.

NOTHING IS MORE POWERFUL THAN PRIVACY.

Privacy is the key to everything.

You can't destroy what you don't know exists.
No one can sabotage what they can't see.
No one can interfere with what's never been spoken.

Your peace, your plans, your relationships, your next moves—they're safest when they're kept private.

Privacy protects the things you value most.
It shields your progress, your growth, and your personal world from unnecessary noise and outside energy.

You don't owe the world access to your every move.
Let them see the results, not the process.

Because when you protect your privacy, you protect your power.

Stop being mad at the winners.

Get real about your effort.

Some people have never been successful at anything they've tried.

And that's tough for them to live with. So instead of taking accountability, they sit back and get mad at the winners—at the people who are doing the work and making things happen.

Most of the time, the people they're mad at don't even know it. They're too busy building, creating, and grinding.

Social media has convinced everyone they're supposed to be a winner, but it hasn't convinced them to actually work for it. So when someone else wins, it triggers something.
"How did they do that?"
"Why not me?"

But the truth is, the answer isn't in someone else's success. It's in your own effort.
If everything you've tried hasn't worked, maybe the real issue isn't them . . . it's you.

And the person people are mad at?
Half the time, it's not even real. It's just a projection of the success they haven't created for themselves.

So stop being mad at the winners. Start getting real with yourself. Because the work you're avoiding is the life you're waiting on.

Drip, jewelry, and cars don't stream!

Good Music Does!

We're living in a time where the music industry feels more focused on image than sound.

But no amount of rented jewelry, flashy cars, or staged homes can cover up weak music.

At the end of the day, music still matters most.

I tell artists all the time:
Before you flex, focus.
Before you try to look like a star,
make sure your music sounds like one.

Because all the flash in the world won't matter if your songs don't connect.

All that extra? It's temporary.
But good music? That stands the test of time.

So stop chasing the look.
Start creating the sound.
Because nothing shines longer than a real hit.

There's always someone willing to work harder & cheaper.

NEVER GET Comfortable!

There's always someone willing to work harder for less.

Too many people land a position and
assume they're irreplaceable.
They stop pushing.
They stop improving.
They start coasting.

But the truth is, in a world with billions of people, you're not the only one who can do what you do.

There's always someone out there who's hungrier, more focused, more skilled or willing to do the same job for less.

And when that person shows up, it's a wake-up call.
By then, it might be too late.

Don't wait for competition to remind you of your value.
Sharpen your skills. Stay consistent. Keep evolving.

Because the moment you get too comfortable is the moment you risk losing everything you took for granted.

Nanny once said,

"WHEN YOU STOP MOVING, YOU STOP MOVING."

Nanny always had a way of dropping gems without even trying. I remember calling her one day while she was out in downtown Philly.

I said, "Nanny, what you doing down there? Did you drive?"

She said, "No baby, I didn't drive, I gotta move around."

I laughed and said,
"Nanny, come on now, sit down and relax."
And she hit me with something I'll never forget:

"All my friends are gone.
But I'm still here 'cause I keep moving.
When you stop moving . . . you stop moving.
And I ain't ready to stop."

That stuck with me.

Keep moving: physically, mentally, spiritually. Because once you stop, everything else starts slowing down too.

Stop Asking For Permission To Live!

Get out of that prison!

Stop asking for permission. Break out of the mental prison.

Some of the most confined people are walking free. Not behind bars, but trapped in mental prisons boxed in by fear, doubt, and the need for approval.

Too many people are stuck, waiting for validation. Waiting for someone to say, "Go ahead, you can do it." But here's the truth: It's your life.

And you don't need permission to live it.

Stop looking to people who aren't in control of their own lives to cosign yours.

Stop delaying your dreams, your growth, your purpose because you're afraid to step outside the box they put you in.

You're already free.
Now go live like it.

If they're the victim in every story—

RUN!

If every story they tell you ends with "somebody did me wrong" or "it wasn't my fault," pay close attention.

Chances are, they weren't the victim—they were the victimizer. And the people they tried to manipulate, lie to, or take advantage of finally caught on and flipped the script.

You can't be the innocent one in every situation. If drama follows someone from job to job, relationship to relationship, and friendship to friendship—and it's always someone else's fault? Believe the pattern, not the pity.

Because truth is, they were probably being shady, selfish, or slick . . .

And when they got exposed, they rewrote the story to protect their image.

So if someone always plays the victim but never takes accountability, don't stick around to become their next story.

Run. Fast.

I stay away from people who are too cautious; they can paralyze you.

Overly cautious people can stilt your progress.

These are the people who always have
a reason not to move.
They'll shoot down your ideas before
they're even fully out of your mouth.
"That won't work." "Don't try that."
"You sure you wanna do that?"

They're quick to say no, but slow to ever
build anything of their own.

Truth is, overly cautious people rarely take risks,
so they rarely accomplish anything.

And if you stick around them too long,
their fear becomes your fear.

Why would you take advice from someone
who's never stepped out on faith?

Why keep company with people who only see
problems, not possibilities?

If you want to grow, evolve, and win, surround yourself with movers, not doubters. Because people who fear everything will stop you from doing anything.

PLEASE START DOING

& your doing will figure everything out for you. Stop being scared.

Life is shorter than we all think!

Truth is, I didn't know what I was doing, but I started anyway.

I wasn't an expert. I didn't have it all figured out.
I just started moving.
And that movement? It turned into momentum.
That momentum turned into success.

So here's my message to you: Just start.
Stop overthinking. Stop waiting. Stop letting fear talk you out of motion.

Back in the day, Nike had it right: Just Do It.
Because when you're doing something, the right people, the right energy, the right information—they start showing up.
Opportunities find you when you're in motion.
And success becomes a byproduct of consistent action.

I didn't have the perfect blueprint.
I just knew I couldn't stay stuck.
So I created motion, and everything I needed met me on the way.

Start where you are.
Use what you have.
And trust that clarity will come through the doing, not the planning.

AIN'T NOTHING PRETTY ABOUT PRETTY PRIVILEGE!

Pretty privilege isn't always what it seems.

A lot of people will want to lay you down,
but very few will want to lift you up.

Being attractive might open doors, but not all of them lead anywhere good.

That so-called pretty privilege often comes with hidden intentions.

People may compliment you, chase you, or offer attention, but too often, it's not about respect, support, or real value. It's about what they can get from you, not how they can pour into you.

So be cautious. Be aware.
Protect your energy, and don't confuse attention for admiration.

Pretty can get you seen but substance is what keeps you respected.

Stay sharp.
Stay grounded.
And know your worth runs deeper than looks.

MONEY AIN'T GOT TIME AND TIME AIN'T GOT MONEY!

Money doesn't have time and time doesn't always have money.

People always say, "Just give me your time."
But the truth is, if you're out there chasing your goals, building something real, and trying to create wealth, your time is limited.

Why?
Because everything in this world costs.
Nothing is free.
Not success.
Not comfort.
Not even peace.

If you're truly grinding to build a future, you won't have endless time to give.

And on the flip side, if you've got too much time on your hands, chances are . . . you're not stacking much money.

It's a trade-off.
The journey to financial freedom requires focus, discipline, and sacrifice.
So before you demand someone's time, understand the cost of building something meaningful.

You can't have both unlimited time and unlimited money. Choose your season and move accordingly.

RESPECT TODAY & TODAY WILL RESPECT YOU.

Don't fumble opportunities by sticking to moves that never helped you win.

Too many people fumble opportunities and relationships because they're still stuck in yesterday's mindset, using moves that never worked.

They're addicted to shortcuts, chasing fast wins, and holding on to habits that never brought success.

Let's be real, if you never won with it before, what makes you think it's going to work now?

We live in a time where people think being slick is being smart. But there's a big difference between strategy and shortcuts.

You can't cheat your way to a better body without the work. You can't become a top-tier talent by sitting out on the grind. You can't finesse your way into greatness.

You have to respect the process.
Show up. Be consistent.
And let go of everything that's been holding you back.

Because the truth is:
You won't reach the next level by trying to finesse it.
You'll only get there by earning it.

BE REALISTIC WITH THE HAND YOU GOT,

not the hand you dream of having.

Play the hand you've got. Not the one you wish you had.

There's a big difference between dreaming and dealing with reality. Too many people miss out on real opportunities because they're living in la-la land, waiting on the life they think they should have, instead of working with the one they've got.

They fumble people, places, and chances because they're playing a game with a hand they don't hold.
You have to be real with yourself.
Maybe your credit's messed up.
Maybe you're behind on rent.
Maybe you're rebuilding, starting over, or just trying to figure it out.

And that's okay. But don't ignore your reality by pretending you're somewhere you're not.
Own where you are. Handle what's in front of you.
And build from there.

Because when you embrace your truth, that's when doors start to open.

The life you want starts with being honest about the one you're in. So stop bluffing.
Play your hand and play it well.

MONEY CHANGES PRINCIPLES.

Money can change principles because money is a monster.

Money has the power to shift people, completely.
It can make them abandon their values, their beliefs, their morals, and everything they once stood for.

I've watched people who had structure, rules, and strong convictions throw it all away the moment money showed up. What once mattered no longer did.
What they once said they'd never do?
Suddenly, it's negotiable.

That's the thing about money:
It's a different kind of force.
It doesn't just test your character . . .
it **exposes** it.

So when you get it, stay grounded.
Because money isn't just paper, it's pressure.
And if you're not solid,
it'll shift everything about you.

I LOVE YOU & I WANT YOU TO WIN!

PLEASE LOVE ME & WANT ME TO WIN!

Please love me enough to want the same for me.

When I say I love you, it means I'm rooting for you.
I want you to win in every way: mentally, emotionally, spiritually, financially.

Your growth, your peace, your success . . .
I want all of that for you.

And all I ask is that you give that same energy back.
You don't have to buy me things or do anything extra.
Just care enough to want to see me win too.
Encourage me. Support me.
Be in my corner the same way I'm in yours.

Because love isn't just a feeling, it's a reciprocated effort. So if I'm showing up for you, I just need to know you'll show up for me too.

REAL LOVE IS GRAM-FREE!

It don't have to prove anything to strangers! It's only about two people!

It doesn't need to prove anything to strangers.
It doesn't need a post, a picture, or a caption to be real.

In today's social media world,
people confuse visibility with validation.
They believe if love isn't broadcast, it doesn't exist.
"If I don't post you, I don't love you."
"If I don't show every date, every moment,
every hug, then it must not be real."

But that's not love. That's performance.

Real love is private, solid, and rooted in connection.
It's about two people being transparent,
loyal, and committed—off the timeline.
It's about building something that doesn't need likes or comments to feel secure.

Because the strongest love isn't for the internet to see.
It's for the two people who show up for each other when no one's watching.

ALWAYS PROTECT

the people who helped you win.

Never forget the ones who lifted you when you were down, supported you when no one else did, and stood by you when you had nothing to offer but potential.

In a world full of noise, gossip, and manipulation, don't let anyone put a battery in your back to turn against the very people who believed in you first.

People will try to rewrite your story, twist your loyalty, or plant doubt in your mind. Don't fall for it.
Because the truth is, not everyone shows up for you when you're in the dark. But those who do? They deserve your protection, your respect, and your gratitude.

Keep them close.
Defend them in rooms they're not in.
And never let temporary voices make you forget permanent support.

THE HATERS ARE PART OF THE JOURNEY,

but don't you ever let them take you off your game.

You'll never see a real hater
sitting next to you at the bank,
in first class, closing deals, or
living well at five-star hotels.
They don't show up in progress,
success, or growth. They only
show up online, in comments,
and in low-vibrational conversations.

Their goal?
To distract you.
To pull you off your path.
To make you react, so you lose focus on the
very thing that's making you win.

Don't give them that power.

Going back and forth with a hater
doesn't elevate you. It platforms them.
They thrive off your attention, not your success.

So let them work. Let them talk.
And most importantly, let them stay where they are,
while you keep going where they can't follow.

STAY FOCUSED ON WHAT'S IMPORTANT.

Everything doesn't warrant a response.

KEEP MOVING FORWARD!

Stay focused on what truly matters, not everything deserves your energy.

Not everything needs to be addressed.
Not every comment, rumor, or opinion requires a response.
The more time you spend trying to explain yourself, defend yourself, or prove something to people who don't matter, the further you drift from your purpose.

Every time you shift focus to negativity, you're stealing energy away from your goals.

And over time, that distraction adds up.
Your progress slows,
your consistency slips,
and before you know it, you're offtrack.

Remember:
You don't have to attend every argument you're invited to.
You don't have to explain yourself to people committed to misunderstanding you.

Protect your focus because your future depends on it.

THERE'S A LOT OF AMAZING, GOOD-HEARTED PEOPLE IN THIS WORLD.

Don't let the few that did you wrong destroy your outlook on people.

There are still good people in this world. Don't let a few bad ones change your heart.

Yes, some people will hurt you, betray you, or disappoint you, but don't let those few experiences make you paranoid or closed off to everyone.

Too many people miss out on genuine connections because they're still holding on to the pain of those who didn't love them right in the past.

So when good people show up, they can't even embrace them. They keep their guard up, expecting the worst—when in reality, the best is right in front of them.
Don't let yesterday's hurt block today's blessings.

There are far more kind, loving, and solid people in this world than there are bad ones.
And truthfully? More good things will happen in your life than bad, if you stay open to receiving them.

Heal. Trust again. And remember,
protecting your heart doesn't mean closing it.

JUST DO THINGS THE RIGHT WAY!

The slick shit is always gonna have you starting over in life!

Do it the right way. The slick route will always set you back.

Take it from someone who tried to cut corners.
I used to look for shortcuts, tried to finesse the system, move slick, and every time, it landed me right back at square one, or worse, in a prison cell.

Nothing ever worked out the way I thought it would. What felt like a fast track ended up being a setback.

The truth is, doing it the right way might take longer but it lasts longer.

And if you mess up? Cool. Just stay focused and keep pushing forward the right way.

Let go of that slick mentality.
Finessing might bring quick wins,
but it always comes with longer losses.

Move with integrity.
Build it solid.
Because the right way is the only way that really works.

STOP LISTENING TO THE PEOPLE WHO TEACH YOU HOW TO LOSE WHAT YOU GOT.

You ain't noticing they don't have shit going on.

Stop taking advice from people who teach you how to lose.

Pay attention. Most of the people trying to talk you out of your position don't have anything going on themselves.

They're not building.
They're not elevating.
They're just close to you, maybe a friend,
a family member, or someone who's always around . . .
but never really moving forward.

And because they're not doing anything with their life, they're quick to offer advice that'll mess up yours.

They'll try to plant doubt, encourage reckless decisions, or talk you into walking away from opportunities they wish they had.

Stop listening to people who've never had what you're trying to build. Protect your progress.

And only take advice from those who know how to keep what they've earned.

EGO IS THE BIGGEST KILLER of LOVE!

Ego ruins everything, but love especially.

It convinces you that you're always right, even when you're clearly wrong.

It blocks accountability, shuts down vulnerability, and turns connection into competition.

Ego doesn't want to compromise.
It doesn't want to apologize.
It would rather protect pride than protect
the person you love.

And slowly but surely, it chips away at the trust, the intimacy, and the foundation of the relationship . . .
all to avoid saying "I messed up" or "Let's fix this."

Love can't survive where ego leads.
If you truly care, put your pride down
before it costs you everything.

IT'S NOT HOW OLD YOU ARE,

it's how old you feel!

Age isn't just a number. It's a mindset.

Some people grow older and start slowing down, not because their body demands it but because their mind does.
They accept limits.
They give up on goals.
They stop dreaming, exploring, and evolving.

That's what makes you old, not the years, but the mindset.

If you still have the drive to grow, the energy to move, the passion to live, and the will to try, you're still young.

Stay active.
Stay curious.
Stay positive.
Take care of your body and your spirit.

Because age will touch your body eventually, but it's your mind that decides whether you keep living or just start existing.

SLOW DOWN.

STOP RUSHING.

BE PRESENT AND ENJOY THE LIFE YOU HAVE.

I finally slowed down because I realized I was rushing to die.

For a long time, I was living in overdrive.
Working nonstop.
Grinding endlessly.
So focused on chasing success,
fixing my past, and becoming someone better . . .
that I forgot to actually live.

I didn't know how to pause. I didn't know how to enjoy life. I was stuck in this mindset of "keep going, don't stop, prove yourself."

But in reality, I wasn't living—I was just moving fast . . .
toward burnout, toward emptiness, toward the end.

At some point, I had to ask myself:
What am I running from? And the answer was . . .
the version of me I used to be.
But the truth is, you can't heal by outrunning your past.
You heal by slowing down, being present, and allowing yourself to enjoy this life while you have it.

So I made a choice:
To stop rushing.
To breathe.
To feel.
And to finally live.

Conversations become promotion.

GIVE 'EM SOMETHING TO ARGUE ABOUT,

and let the noise do the work.

Give them something to argue about, then let them talk.

In today's world, especially on social media, controversy is marketing.

When people start debating your name, your message, or your moves—that's free promotion.

Let them argue. Let them repost. Let them disagree.

You don't need to interrupt or defend yourself. Because every conversation they have is more attention, more visibility, more reach.

Sometimes all it takes is saying what you truly believe and boom, the conversation takes off.

Now you're being discussed in rooms you've never been in.

Don't fight it.
Let the noise do the work.
Because when they're arguing about you, they're advertising you.

LIFE IS SIMPLE, WAKE UP EVERY DAY & LIVE.

Life will guide you if you let it.

Don't overcomplicate it.

You don't have to have everything figured out.
Just get up, be present, and let life do what it does:
teach you, guide you, and shape you.

Every day is a new lesson.
Some days you'll laugh, some days you'll learn,
and some days you'll simply listen.

But the key is to keep showing up with no pressure,
just presence.

Some mornings I wake up not knowing what the day holds,
but I know I'll get something out of it.
And that's what matters.

Wake up.
Live.
Learn.
Laugh.
And let life teach you as you go.

Not everyone can join your journey toward success.

Accept the fact and stay focused on the goal.

You're only entitled to what you work for. Not what you're around for.

On the road to success, you'll lose friends.
You'll grow apart from family.
And the painful part? Many of them will expect something from you, simply because they know you, not because they contributed to your journey or believed in your vision.

But here's the truth: You don't owe anyone what they didn't help build.

As you elevate, you'll want to bring everyone with you.
You'll think, "I made it—I want them to make it too."
But sometimes, trying to carry people who won't carry themselves will only weigh you down.

It's hard. It hurts. But everybody can't go.
Some people aren't meant to take the ride with you because they never prepared for the destination.

And if you force it, you'll end up enabling them, draining yourself, and risking everything you worked for.

Protect your progress.
Move with love but move with wisdom.
Because success requires sacrifice, and sometimes that means letting go of people who only know how to take.

A LIMITED MENTALITY WON'T ALLOW YOU TO GROW.

A limited mentality will keep you stuck.

That mindset might have helped you survive,
but it won't help you grow.

That way of thinking doesn't translate into every part of life—especially not in business, relationships, or personal development.

It limits your perspective, your opportunities, and your ability to evolve.

Some people stay stuck in it because it's familiar.
It feels real, it feels loyal, it feels safe.
But in reality, it's just a cycle that blocks progress.

If you can't let go of the street mentality, you'll never fully step into your potential.

Growth requires a mindset shift.
And sometimes that means unlearning the very survival tactics that once kept you afloat, so you can finally rise.

***STOP ASKING FOR THE OPINIONS OF PEOPLE* WHO HAVE ALREADY QUIT.**

You've seen people you care about and admire wave the white flag.

They quit on themselves.
They stopped believing it was possible.
So why are you still seeking guidance, encouragement, or validation from them?

If they didn't believe it could happen for them,
what makes you think they'll believe it can happen for you?

It's not hate.
It's not malice.
They just gave up and now they can't give you what they no longer carry: hope, drive, or vision.

Be mindful of who you take direction from.
Because advice from someone who quits will always lead you back to where they stopped.

During your one time on this planet, do something that will live longer than you.

BUILD LEGACY.

You only get one life. Do something that outlives you.

Every day is a chance to create something
that will live beyond your time here.

Legacy isn't about being perfect, it's about being intentional.

The greatest people we still talk about, 10, 20,
even 100 years later, left something behind.
They created.
They inspired.
They moved the world forward in their own way.

They chose to be extraordinary while they were here.

And you can do the same.
Your words, your work, your impact, it can outlive you.

Make your time count.
Create something timeless.
And leave this world better than you found it.

Unlimited >>

ACCESS BREEDS

Entitlement.

The more access people have to you, the more they start believing they're owed what you've worked for.

They think being around you means they should receive the same blessings as you.

You get a new car, they want one.
You take a trip, they expect an invite.
You elevate, they feel entitled to rise with you . . . without doing the work.

That's why unlimited access is dangerous. When people confuse proximity with ownership, they start feeling entitled to benefits that were never meant for them.

Protect your peace.
Protect your progress.
And most importantly, protect your access.
Not everyone should be that close to what you're building.

STAY FAR AWAY FROM GOSSIPERS.

They are the creators of confusion and chaos.

Gossipers are quietly dangerous.

Gossipers don't just talk, they twist.
They take pieces of truth, add their own spin,
and create confusion wherever they go.

They live for drama.
They stir up tension.
And they'll say anything just to have something to say,
even if it means tearing someone down.

These are the people who break up families,
ruin friendships, damage relationships, and
destroy business connections . . . all with their words.

They are the creators of chaos and they often smile
while doing it.

Protect your space.
Protect your energy.
And keep gossip far from your circle because
once they talk about others to you, they'll talk
about you to others.

Sometimes

YOU HAVE TO DOWN-GRADE TO UPGRADE.

Let go of what's holding you back,
even if it looks good on the outside.

Sometimes that means releasing the car,
the apartment, the image, or even the people
who no longer serve your growth.

There's nothing wrong with stepping back if it helps
you step forward the right way.

A setback can give you clarity.
It can show you what wasn't working and create
space for something better.

Don't let pride keep you stuck.

Less now can lead to way more later
if you're willing to let go to grow.

WRITE DOWN

The house you want: ______________________________

Car you want: ______________________________

Account balance you want: ______________________________

Relationship you want: ______________________________

Love you want: ______________________________

Friends you want: ______________________________

Places you want to go: ______________________________

Life you want: ______________________________

Everything you want is waiting for you as long as you believe it is!

Write it all down . . .

The house you want.
The car you want.
The account balance you want.
The relationship, the love, the friendships,
the places you want to experience.
Even the advice and guidance you're hoping for,
it's all possible.

But first, you have to claim it.
And that starts with writing it down.

I always ask people, "Do you have the list?"
And they look at me, confused.
"What list?"
The list of what you want in life.

If you don't have one, how are you supposed to know what you're working toward? How do you measure progress if you haven't defined the destination?

Without a list, you're just floating.
With it, you've got direction.

So write it down. Define your vision.
And remind yourself daily: This is what I'm building.

Because everything you want is already waiting . . .
once you're clear enough to go after it.

The moment you stop explaining yourself is the moment

you start elevating.

One of the clearest signs you're still shrinking is how much you feel the need to explain yourself.

You explain your decisions, your boundaries, your growth, trying to make everyone comfortable with who you're becoming. But alignment doesn't overexplain. It moves.

Overexplaining is often guilt dressed up as politeness. It's people-pleasing. It's fear that your "no" won't be received well. But confidence doesn't beg to be understood.

Not everyone is meant to understand your evolution. Some aren't confused, they're uncomfortable that you've stopped shrinking.

Instead of defending every move, choose distance. Distance protects your peace. Distance preserves your energy.

You don't owe anyone a presentation on your growth.

The moment you stop explaining is the moment you start ascending. Elevation isn't loud. It's decisive. Sometimes the clearest message is silence and space.

Social media didn't ruin your focus.

You handed it over.

Take your power back and log off the lie.

It's easy to blame the app. The algorithm. The endless scroll. But distraction requires permission.

Every time you chose your phone over your work, comparison over confidence—that was a choice. Social media didn't steal your focus. You gave it access.

And if you handed it over, you can take it back.

The real danger isn't the app—it's the illusion. The illusion that everyone's ahead. That you're behind. That loud means successful.

You're comparing your real life to someone else's edited highlight reel—which is a lie.

Focus is currency. Attention is power. And you've been spending both carelessly.

So log off—not forever, but long enough to remember who you are without the noise.

Because the moment you stop feeding the illusion is the moment you start feeding your future.

Take your power back. Your life is waiting off-screen.

You're not
overwhelmed.
You're
undisciplined.

Put it in the right bucket or drop it.

We love saying we're "overwhelmed."
It sounds harmless—like life is just happening to us.

But most overwhelm isn't about volume.
It's about lack of structure.

You're saying yes to too much. Mixing priorities with distractions. Treating everything like it matters equally. That's not overwhelm—that's chaos.

Discipline isn't doing more.
It's deciding what deserves your energy.

Put it in the right bucket:
Does it grow your future?
Protect your peace?
Move your goals forward?
If it doesn't, why are you carrying it?

A lot of what exhausts you is optional—drama, distractions, commitments you didn't need to accept.

Sometimes the power move isn't managing everything.

It's dropping what was never yours.
Put it in the right bucket. Or let it go.

You've learned to say yes to yourself and no to everything that distracts you.

Saying yes to yourself isn't selfish.
It's alignment.

Every distraction you release creates space for clarity.
Every boundary you set sharpens your focus.
Every "no" protects the future you're building.

When you stop giving energy to what pulls you off course, you finally have the power to pour into what moves you forward.

Choose you.
Choose growth.
And watch how everything else begins to fall into place.

THANK YOU

Acknowledgments

First and foremost, I want to thank God. None of this happens without divine alignment, protection, and grace. Every word in this book was guided by something bigger than me. To my family, you're my foundation. You kept me steady when life was heavy and reminded me that love and loyalty are the real success.

To Desiree Ivey, my business partner, creative collaborator, and constant force—you helped turn raw ideas into impact. Your vision, structure, and belief brought this book and every project we build to life. Thank you for always seeing the bigger picture and helping me walk it out.

To my incredible book team and everyone who pours into the Wallo267 mission daily—you are the reason these words move beyond pages and into people's lives. Your dedication and discipline keep this message alive.

To my readers and supporters—the people who quote the words, share the posts, and live the lessons—thank you for trusting my voice. Every story, every DM, every moment of connection reminds me why I do this. And to anyone still fighting to believe in themselves, this book is for you. Keep growing. Keep choosing you. Keep saying no to anything that dims your light.

With love and gratitude, **WALLO267**

About the Author

WALLO267 is proof that purpose has no borders. After serving twenty years behind bars, he turned his story into a global movement of resilience and reinvention. A *New York Times* best-selling author, cultural advisor at YouTube, former chief marketing officer of REFORM Alliance, and co-host of *Million Dollaz Worth of Game* (named by *The Hollywood Reporter* among the most powerful voices in podcasting, 2024), WALLO267 continues to merge impact and innovation. He uses partnerships, like his $4.5 million minority business initiative with Barstool Sports, his lifestyle brand ARPLNSNHOTLS, and his production company Nanny's House Entertainment, which develops and produces movies, TV series, books, and podcasts, to prove your past is data, not destiny.

Keep in Touch with Wallo267

Stay connected, stay inspired, and keep growing with me.

I share news about upcoming releases, daily messages, lessons, and moments to help you stay focused on becoming your best self.

Follow & connect on social:
Instagram • Facebook • TikTok • YouTube • X (Twitter)

@WALLO267

For speaking engagements, partnerships, and media inquiries:

info@wallo267.com

www.wallo267.com

Audiobook available from Nanny's House Publishing wherever audiobooks are sold.

Your journey matters.
Keep showing up for yourself every day.

Hay House Titles of Related Interest

YOU CAN HEAL YOUR LIFE, the movie,
starring Louise Hay & Friends
(available as an online streaming video)
www.hayhouse.com/louise-movie

THE SHIFT, the movie,
starring Dr. Wayne W. Dyer
(available as an online streaming video)
www.hayhouse.com/the-shift-movie

***

PROTECT YOUR PEACE: Nine Unapologetic Principles for Thriving in a Chaotic World, by Trent Shelton

LIVE THE LIFE YOU DESERVE: How to Let Go of What No Longer Serves You and Embody Your Highest Self, by Sylvester McNutt III

7 RULES OF SELF-RELIANCE: How to Stay Low, Keep Moving, Invest in Yourself, and Own Your Future, by Maha Abouelenein

All of the above are available at your local bookstore, or may be ordered by visiting:

Hay House USA: www.hayhouse.com®
Hay House Australia: www.hayhouse.com.au
Hay House UK: www.hayhouse.co.uk
Hay House India: www.hayhouse.co.in

We hope you enjoyed this Hay House book. If you'd like to receive our online catalog featuring additional information on Hay House books and products, or if you'd like to find out more about the Hay Foundation, please contact:

Hay House LLC, P.O. Box 5100, Carlsbad, CA 92018-5100
(760) 431-7695 or (800) 654-5126
www.hayhouse.com® • www.hayfoundation.org

Published in Australia by:
Hay House Australia Publishing Pty Ltd
18/36 Ralph St., Alexandria NSW 2015
Phone: +61 (02) 9669 4299
www.hayhouse.com.au

Published in the United Kingdom by:
Hay House UK Ltd
1st Floor, Crawford Corner,
91–93 Baker Street, London W1U 6QQ
Phone: +44 (0)20 3927 7290
www.hayhouse.co.uk

Published in India by:
Hay House Publishers (India) Pvt Ltd
Muskaan Complex, Plot No. 3,
B-2, Vasant Kunj, New Delhi 110 070
Phone: +91 11 41761620
www.hayhouse.co.in